HOL
My Invisible Friend

For kids too!

By Patricia Holland

About Pat-
https://www.patriciaholland.org/pat-holland/

Copyright 2016, 2023 Patricia Holland

All Rights Reserved

https://www.patriciaholland.org

Contact the author
pat@patriciaholland.org

Dear Reader,

Do you have a favorite verse in the Bible?
One that encourages you, but also makes you sad?

For me, that verse would be 2 Corinthians 13:14.
"The grace of the Lord Jesus Christ, and
the love of God, and the fellowship of
the Holy Spirit be with all of you."

I love this verse, because I have personally experienced
the saving grace of Jesus,
the love of the Father,
and the fellowship of
the Holy Spirit.

It makes me sad because some children know very little about the Holy Spirit. And many have never experienced His Presence personally. For many children, He is a stranger.

And yet, children desperately need the fellowship of the Holy Spirit!

I believe my story can help children know and experience His Presence and fullness personally. Thank you for giving me the opportunity to help your children know Holy Spirit.

God bless you,
Pat

I have an invisible Friend.

Maybe you think I'm too old to have an invisible friend. I said invisible... Not imaginary.

There's a huge difference between those two words.

Some of nature's most powerful forces are invisible.

Electricity.
Gravity.
Wind.

They may be invisible but they are essential for life as we know it.

Your lungs find the invisible and your blood carries it to every cell in your body; and you live.

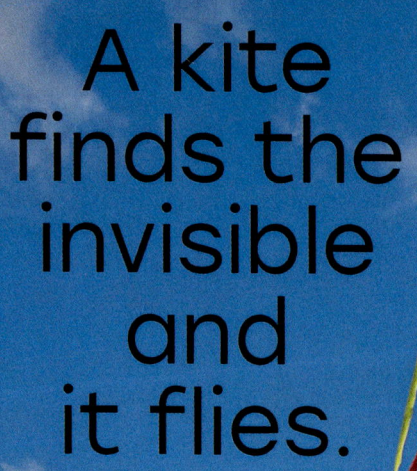

A kite
finds the
invisible
and
it flies.

Try to tell a kid
holding a ball
of string tied
to a twisting,
bobbing kite
high in the sky
that the wind
isn't real;
they'll giggle at
your silliness.

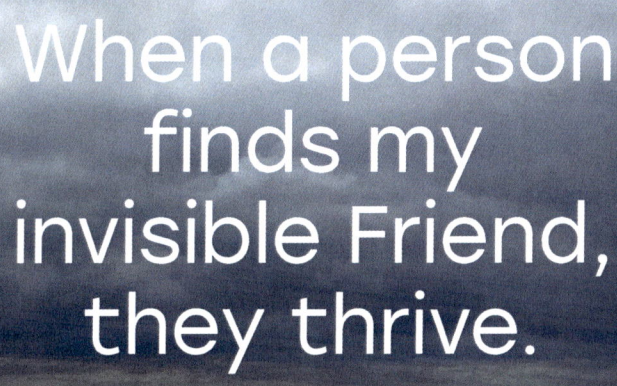

When a person finds my invisible Friend, they thrive.

They know He is **REAL.**

Because He is invisible,
I can't show you
a picture of Him,
but I can tell
you about Him.

Wonderful
doesn't come close
to describing Him!
But it is
a starting point.

In some ways,
He is like
the wind.

Sometimes
the wind is so gentle
it tickles your face.
He is gentle,
so loving,
and very kind.

Sometimes
the wind is strong.
Strong enough to
move things around.

And like the wind,
my Friend
is really strong.

Like the wind fills
a sail and empowers
it to move across the water,

He fills us with His power
to be— to do—to serve.

Think about how hot you get running around on a scorching hot, summer day and how refreshing a cool breeze feels.

Like a cool whisper
of wind on a
hot summer day,

My Wonderful Friend

refreshes
and
renews.

Like the voice of the wind whistling through the leaves, **His voice** instructs, encourages and guides.

We hear **His voice** through the words of Scripture and His gentle whisper in our spirit.

His voice
whispers truths
to help us understand
the Bible better.
He reminds us of
God's promises in Scripture
to encourage us.

Like you can hear and feel
the wind, you can hear and
feel my Precious Friend.

I've given you just a few
of the many reasons that
I think it is so important
to know my special Friend.

His name is

Holy Spirit.

Maybe you're wondering,
"Who is the Holy Spirit?"

You may already know that
God the Father is God.
Jesus is God.
AND the Holy Spirit is God.
Three different personalities

ONE GOD.

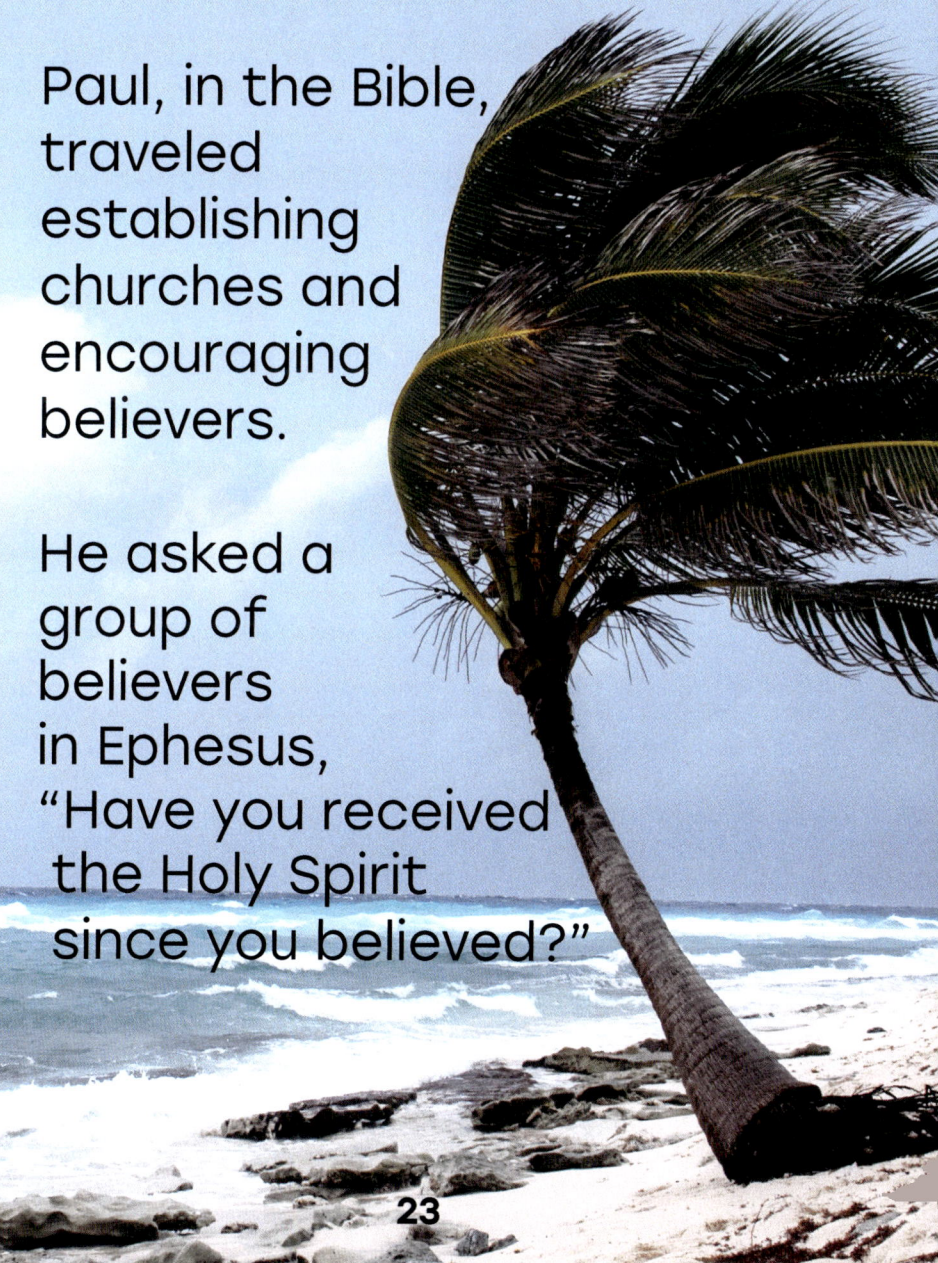

Some Christians in the New Testament asked that same question too!

Paul, in the Bible, traveled establishing churches and encouraging believers.

He asked a group of believers in Ephesus, "Have you received the Holy Spirit since you believed?"

Somebody blurted out, "We didn't even know there was a HOLY SPIRIT."
(Acts 19:1-6)
They knew about Jesus; they just didn't know the rest of the story.

It's important for you to know the rest of the story!

Jesus told His followers that He was going away.
They were confused and heartbroken!

Jesus explained,
"The Father will not send Holy Spirit until I am gone."

"So I must leave you. Wait in Jerusalem until you receive the Father's Gift."

"I've been with you, but Holy Spirit will fill you."

That Promise was fulfilled on the Day of Pentecost.
Read about it in Acts 2 in your Bible.

120 believers were gathered in Jerusalem, just like Jesus told them to do. They were probably praying and worshipping God while waiting.

On the Day of Pentecost, God sent a sound that filled the whole house where they were sitting. It sounded like a mighty wind.

They saw flames of fire, that separated and rested on each person.

And they were filled with the Holy Spirit and began to speak with other tongues as God's Spirit enabled them or gave them the words to speak.

Holy Spirit didn't come to be with them, He came to fill them.

Holy Spirit came to be their
helper and their friend.

Nobody knew that better than
the Apostle Paul.
Paul ended his letter to the
Corinthians with
a powerful challenge.

2 Corinthians 13:14 (BSB)
The grace of the Lord Jesus
Christ, and the love of God, and
the fellowship of the
Holy Spirit
be with all of you.

Did you see that?
"The fellowship of the Holy Spirit."
That's friendship.
Holy Spirit friendship.
He came to be your friend too!

Every believer needs to know that Holy Spirit came to be their friend.

When I was a little girl, I repented and believed on Jesus as my Savior. I attended a good church.

But I didn't know Holy Spirit. When I felt God's Presence, I responded to the pastor's salvation invitation... Again. Again. And **AGAIN!** That's all I knew to do.

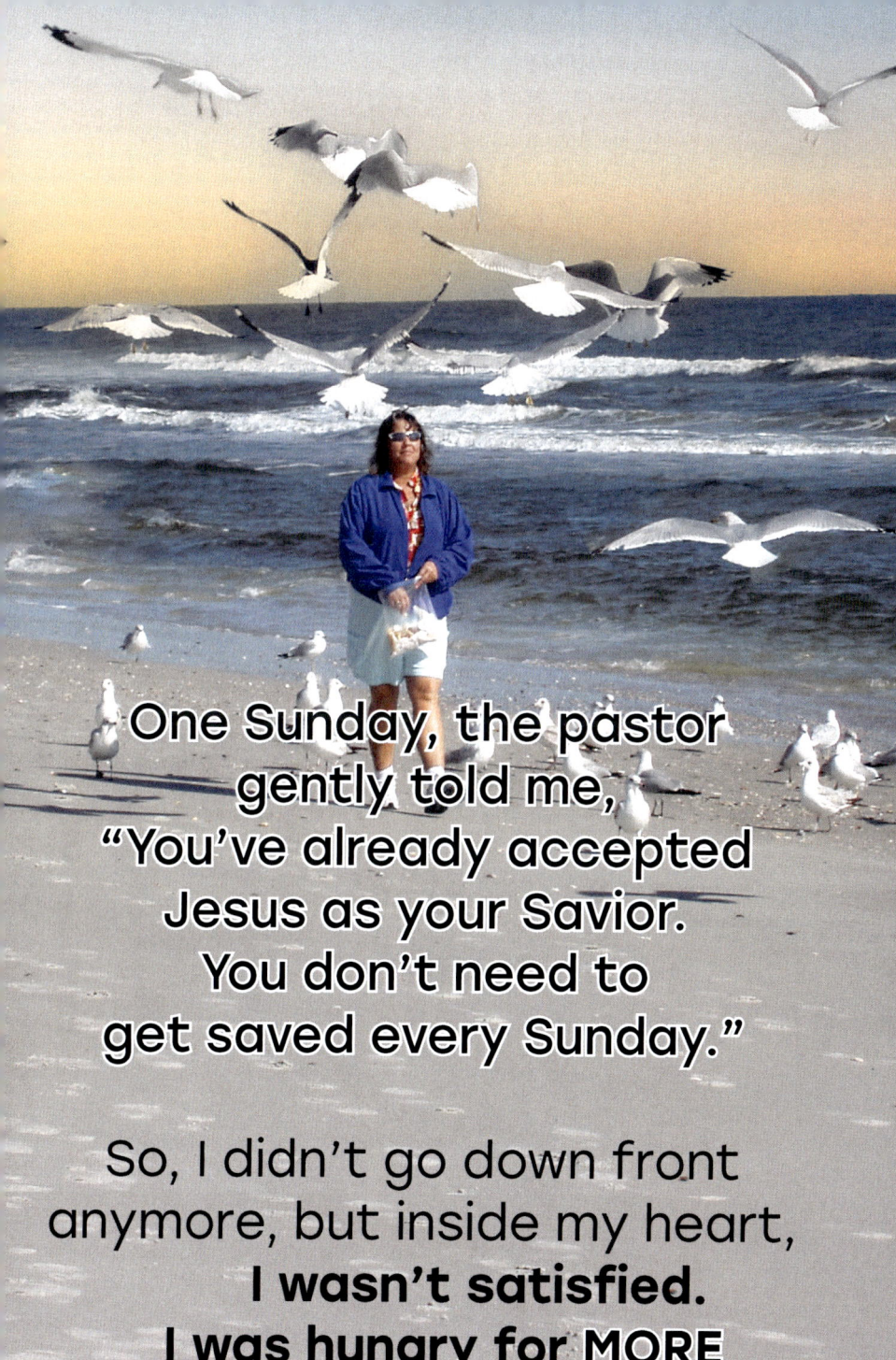

One Sunday, the pastor gently told me, "You've already accepted Jesus as your Savior. You don't need to get saved every Sunday."

So, I didn't go down front anymore, but inside my heart, **I wasn't satisfied. I was hungry for MORE.**

Later, a friend helped
me understand that
I was born of the Spirit
when I believed on Jesus.
And, I could also
be filled with
the Holy Spirit.

God had more for me!
So, I asked. I believed.
And I received **Holy Spirit**.
I yielded to Holy Spirit
and spoke words
that I didn't understand.

If you have believed on Jesus as your Savior, you have been born of God's Spirit.

Do you realize that even children can be filled with the Holy Spirit?
Read Acts 2:39 in your Bible.

And that includes YOU!

Ask.

Read Luke 11:13 in your Bible.
Most people are praying when they receive the Holy Spirit. I hope you will ask God for more of Him. Tell Him that you want His powerful, free gift that
He has offered every believer.

Believe

Some people don't believe that you can be filled with the Holy Spirit. But you can.

Believe that Jesus wants to fill you with the Holy Spirit. Read Galatians 3:14 in your Bible.

Receive

Then begin to worship and praise Jesus right out loud. Don't focus on using the right words, just love on Jesus with words from your heart.

Don't get in a hurry. As you spend time worshipping and loving on Him, you will feel His Presence. His Presence is loving and wonderful.

Yield

Respond to His Presence by speaking the words or syllables He gives you.

It might feel strange to say something you don't understand, but that's OK.
The more you yield to His leading, the easier it will become.

As you spend time with your Wonderful Friend everyday He will help you be more and more like Jesus!

I want to say thank you to some talented photographers:

Pages

10,11	Aaron Burden
12, 13	Boy Adobe Stock
16	Girl by Nathan Seimers
17	Sailboat dejab916
18	Ulrike Mai from Pixabay.com
21	Bible and hands Adobe Stock
22,23	Adobe Stock

Want to know More about the Holy Spirit? I want to give you a free download to remind you of 7 Benefits of Spirit Filled Living "Holy Spirit came to Help You..." with the promise from Scripture Card

www.patriciaholland.org/holy-spirit/

Made in the USA
Monee, IL
06 October 2024